The Classical Piano
Sheet Music Series

INTERMEDIATE
FRENCH
FAVORITES

ISBN 978-1-70512-476-5

HAL•LEONARD®

Visit Hal Leonard Online at
www.halleonard.com

World headquarters, contact:
Hal Leonard
7777 West Bluemound Road
Milwaukee, WI 53213
Email: info@halleonard.com

In Europe, contact:
Hal Leonard Europe Limited
42 Wigmore Street
Marylebone, London, W1U 2RN
Email: info@halleonardeurope.com

In Australia, contact:
Hal Leonard Australia Pty. Ltd.
4 Lentara Court
Cheltenham, Victoria, 3192 Australia
Email: info@halleonard.com.au

Contents

4

The Sewing Machine

(La machine à coudre)

from *Album pour les tout-petits*

Mélanie Bonis
1858–1937
Op. 103, No. 6

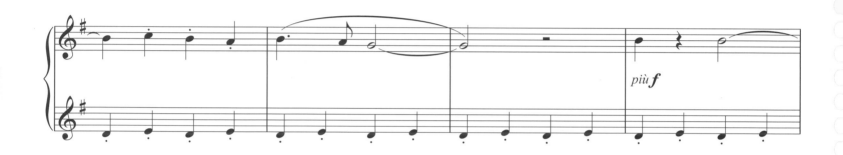

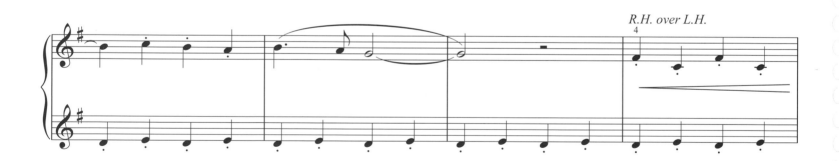

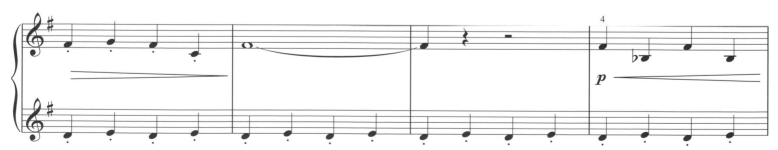

Fingerings are by the composer.

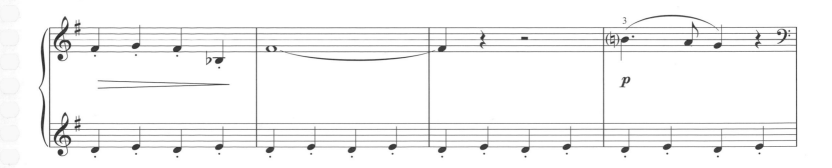

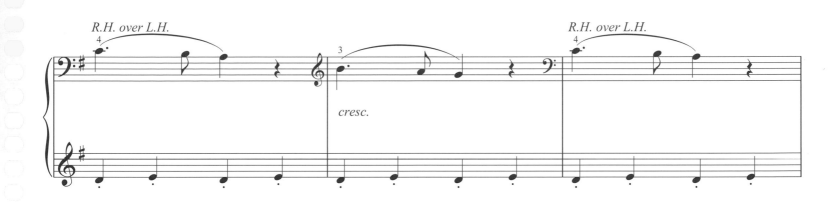

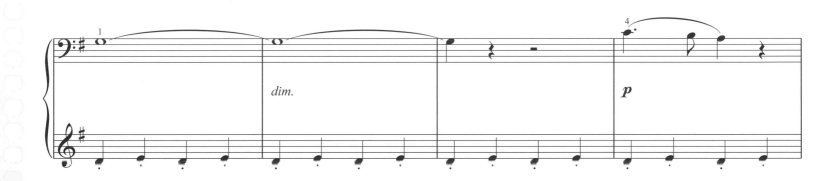

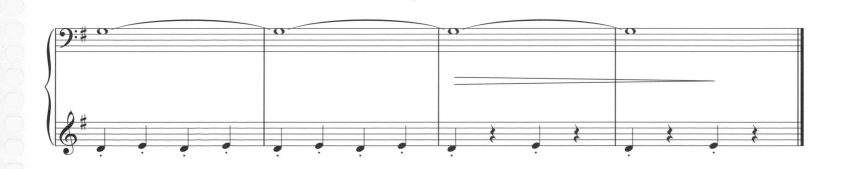

Gavotte in A minor

from *Album d'enfants*, Op. 123, No. 5

Cécile Chaminade
1857–1944

Gigue in C Major

from *Album d'enfants*, Op. 123, No. 6

Cécile Chaminade
1857–1944

Rigaudon in A minor

from *Album d'enfants*, Op. 126, No. 3

Cécile Chaminade
1857–1944

Arabesque No. 1

from *Deux Arabesques*

Claude Debussy
1862–1918

cresc. e poco mosso

Tempo rubato (un peu moins vite)

This page has intentionally been left black to facilitate page turns

Clair de lune
from *Suite Bergamasque*

Claude Debussy
1862–1918

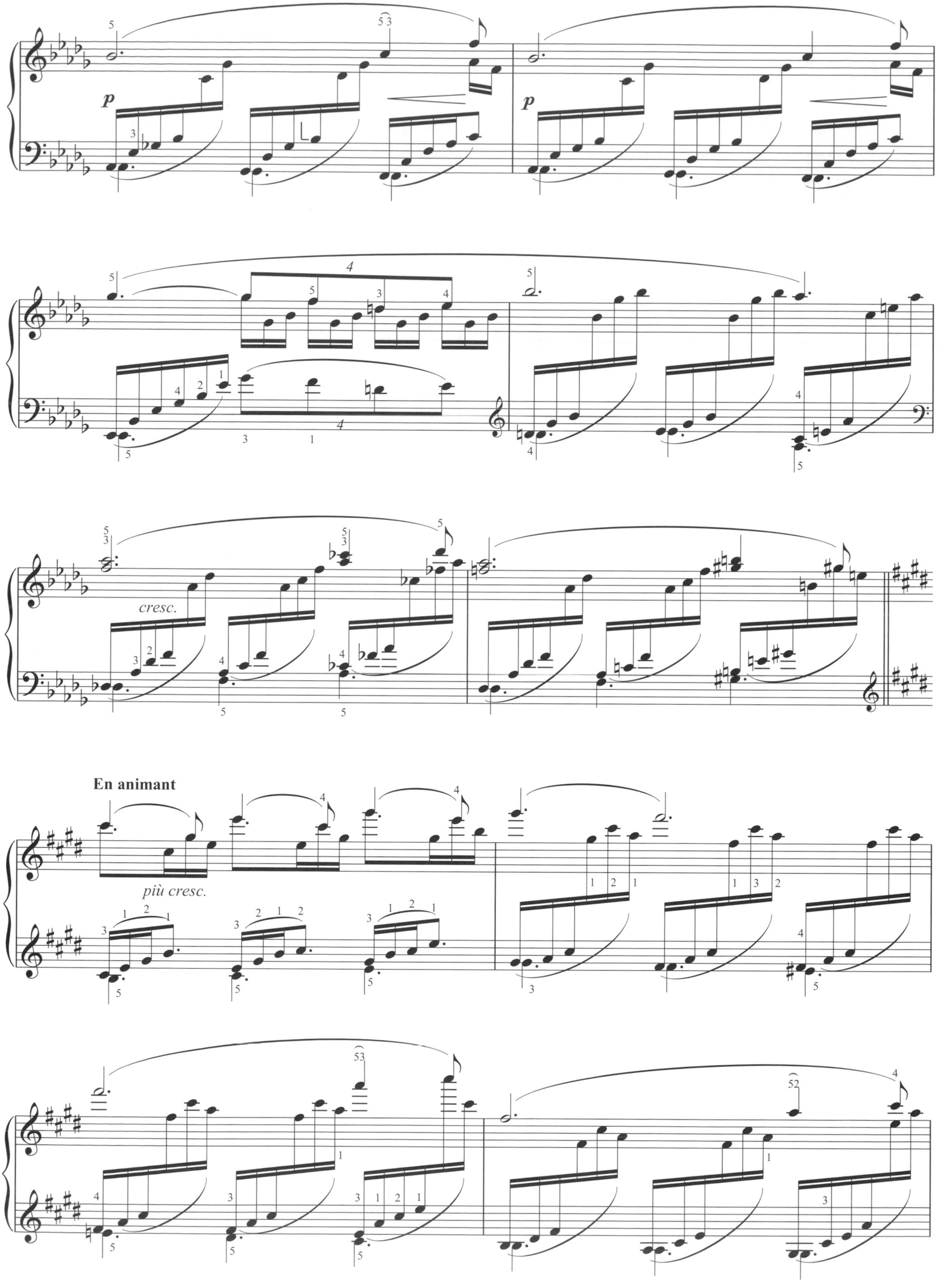
p
p
cresc.
En animant
più cresc.

a Tempo I

pp *morendo jusqu'à la fin*

Doctor Gradus ad Parnassum

from *Children's Corner*

Claude Debussy
1862–1918

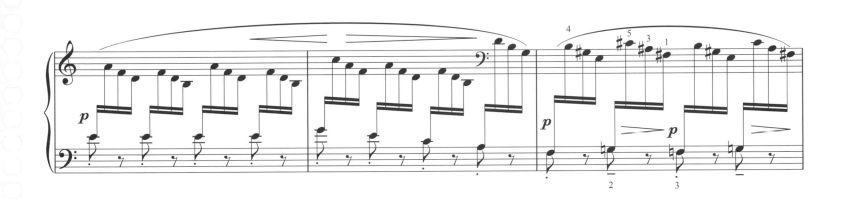

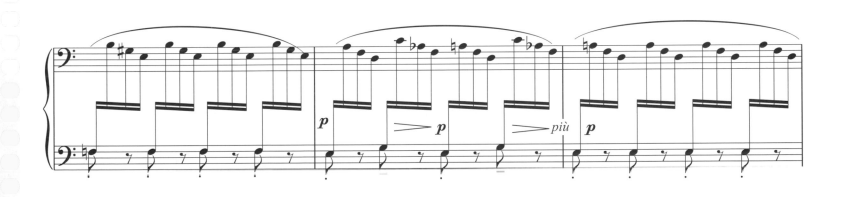

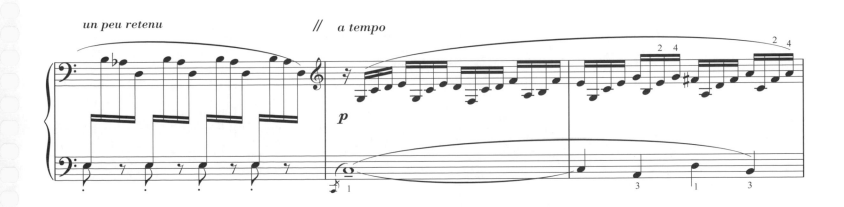

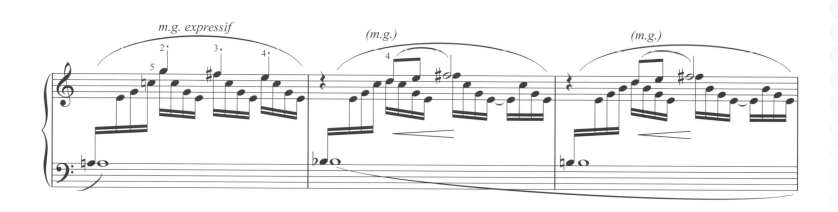

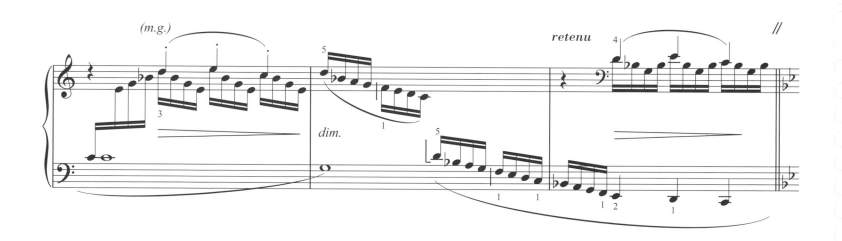

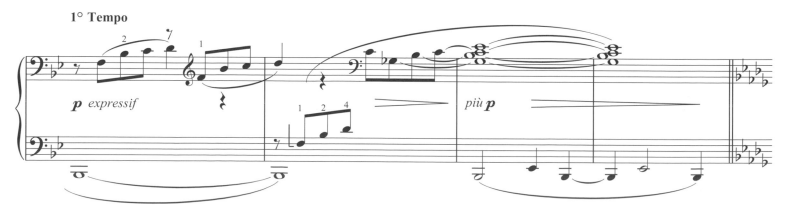

*play with both fingers.

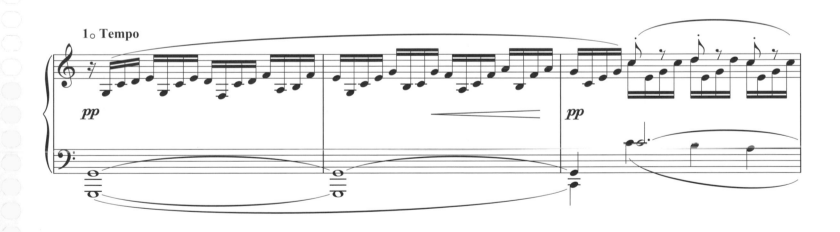

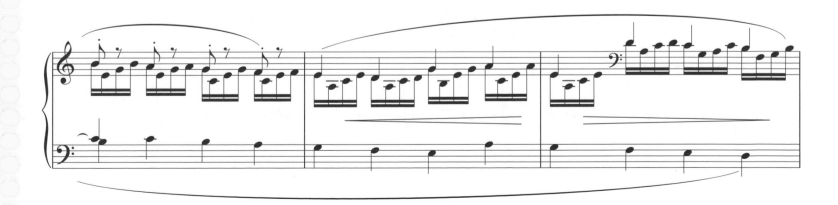

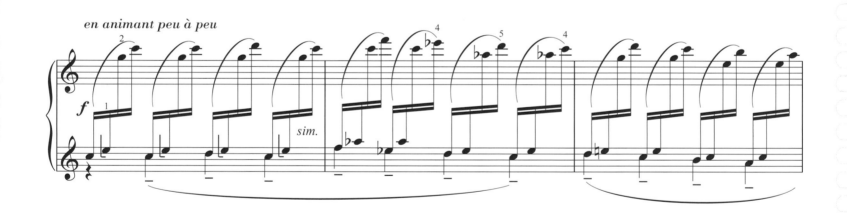

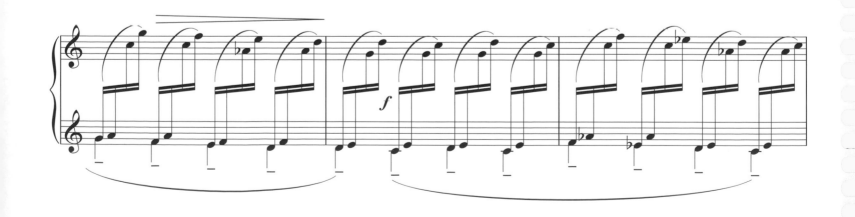

La fille aux cheveux de lin

from *Préludes*, Première Livre

Claude Debussy
1862–1918

Fingerings are by the composer.

Les sons et les parfums tournent dans l'air du soir

Claude Debussy
1862–1918

Cedez

Tranquille et flottant

Tempo

En retenant

Plus retenu

Comme une lointaine sonnerie de cors

Encore plus lointain et plus retenu

Rêverie

Claude Debussy
1862–1918

The little Shepherd
from *Children's Corner*

Claude Debussy
1862–1918

Très modéré

plus mouvementé

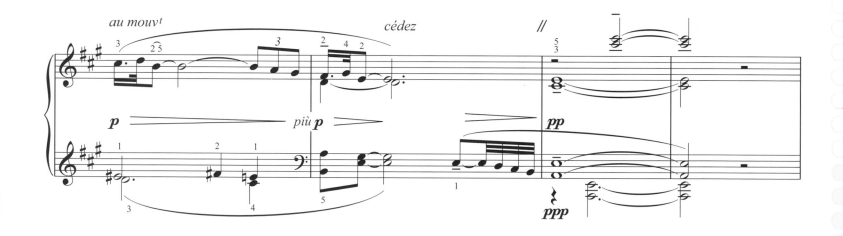

Etude in C Major

from *Vingt cinq études faciles*, Op. 50, No. 1

Louise Dumont Farrenc
1804–1875

Andante grazioso

Etude in A minor

from *Vingt cinq études faciles*, Op. 50, No. 2

Louise Dumont Farrenc
1804–1875

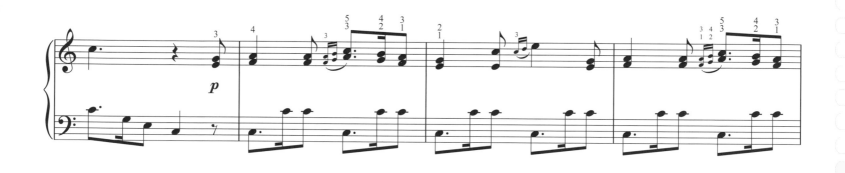

Impromptu in B minor

Louise Dumont Farrenc
1804–1875

Improvisation

from *8 Pièces brèves*, Op. 84, No. 5

Gabriel Fauré
1845–1924

to Madame Florent Saglio

Romance sans paroles
Op. 17, No. 3

Gabriel Fauré
1845–1924

The Doll's Lament
(Les plaintes d'une poupée)

César Franck
1822–1890

à Mademoiselle Jeanne Leleu

Prélude

Maurice Ravel
1875–1937

Assez lent et très expressif (d'un rythme libre) ♩ = 60 environ

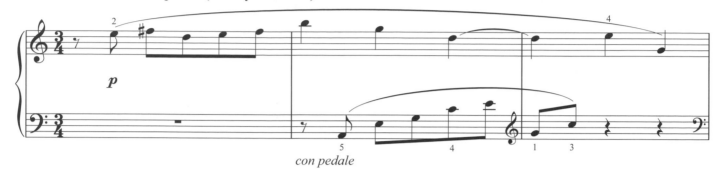

con pedale

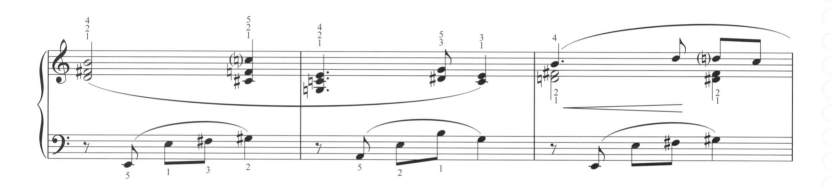

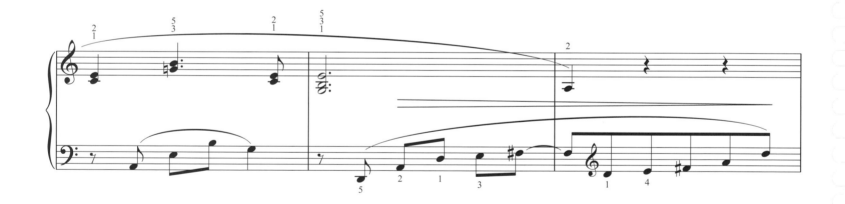

Pavane pour une infante défunte

Maurice Ravel
1875–1937

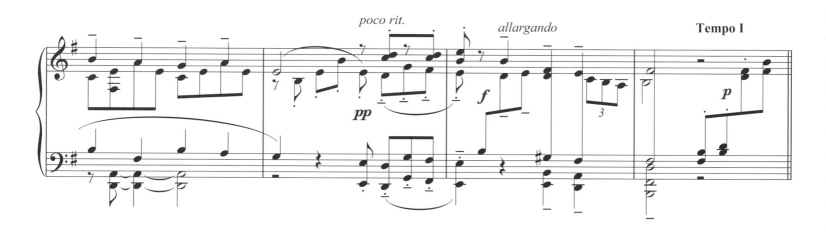

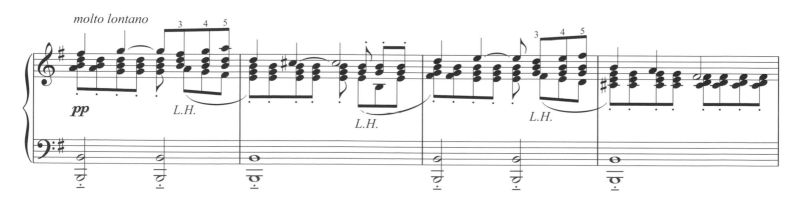

Danse de Travers No. 2

from *Pièces froides*

Erik Satie
1866–1925

Go on [cantabile]

The same

With the corner of the hand

Alone

Be visible for a moment

Blend together

Medium done

Gnossienne No. 1

from *Trois Gnossiennes*

Erik Satie
1866–1925

Lent *(Slowly)*

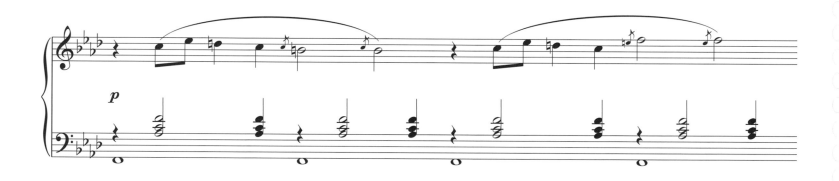

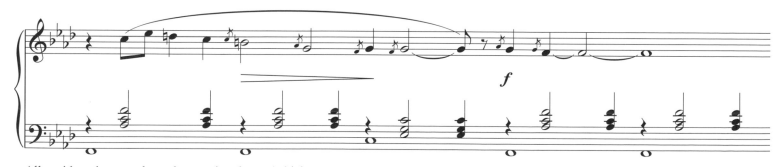

All accidentals carry through an entire phrase (which serves as a "measure").

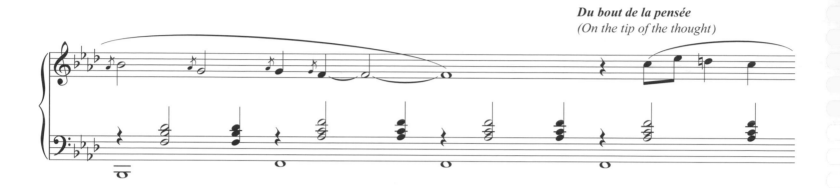

Du bout de la pensée
(On the tip of the thought)

Postulez en vous-même
(Ask yourself)

Pas à pas
(Step by step)

Sur la langue
(On the tip of the tongue)

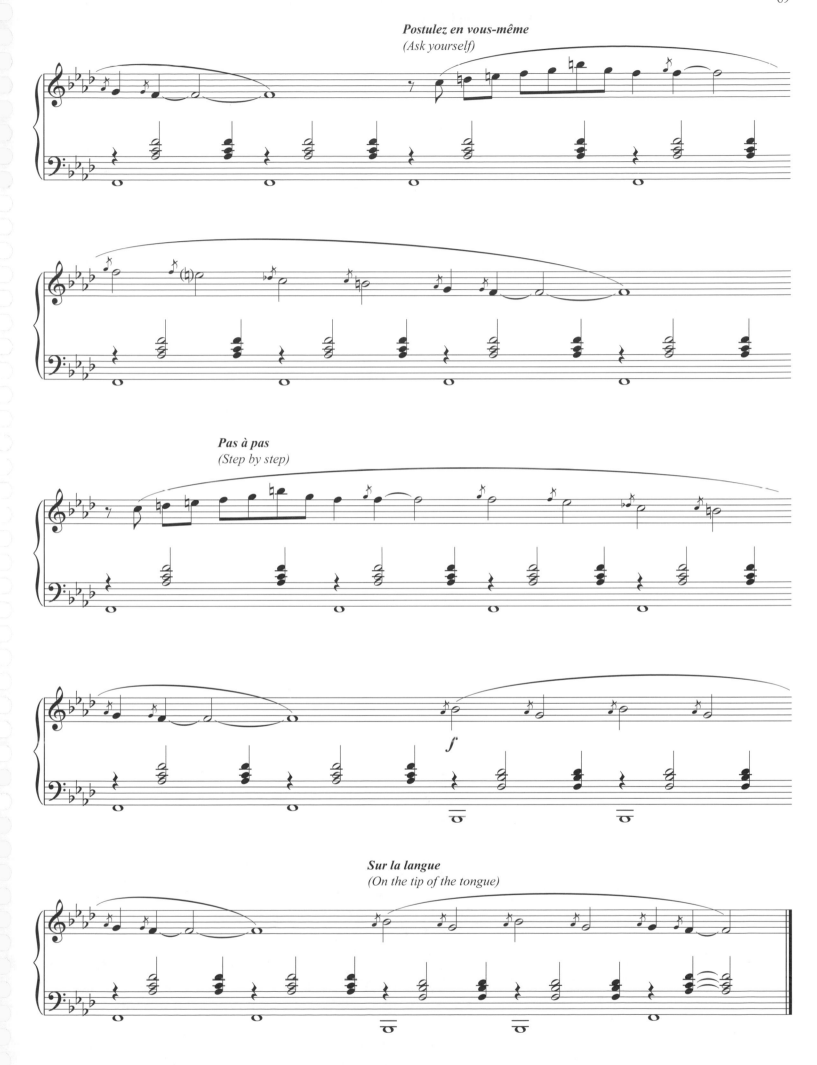

Gnossienne No. 2

from *Trois Gnossiennes*

Erik Satie
1866–1925

Avec étonnement
(With astonishment)

Ne sortez pas
(Don't leave)

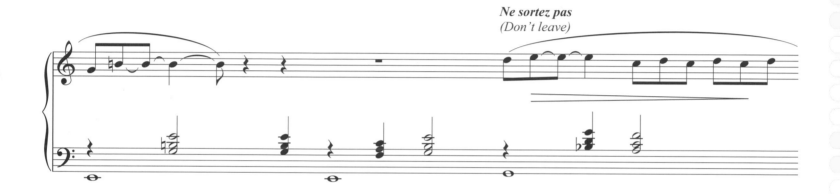

72

Gnossienne No. 3
from *Three Gnossiennes*

Erik Satie
1866–1925

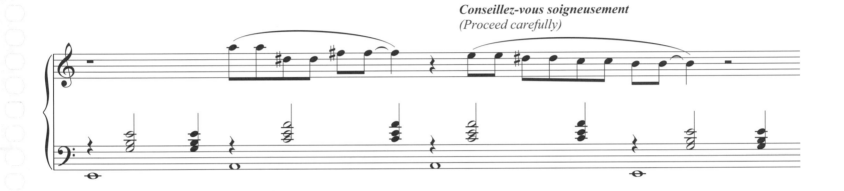

Conseillez-vous soigneusement
(Proceed carefully)

Munissez-vous de clairvoyance
(Arm yourself with clairvoyance)

Seul, pendant un instant
(Alone, for a moment)

De manière à obtenir un creux
(So as to be a hole)

Très perdu
(Very lost)

Portez cela plus loin
(Carry this further away)

Ouvrez la tête
(Open the head)

Enfouissez le son
(Muffle the sound)

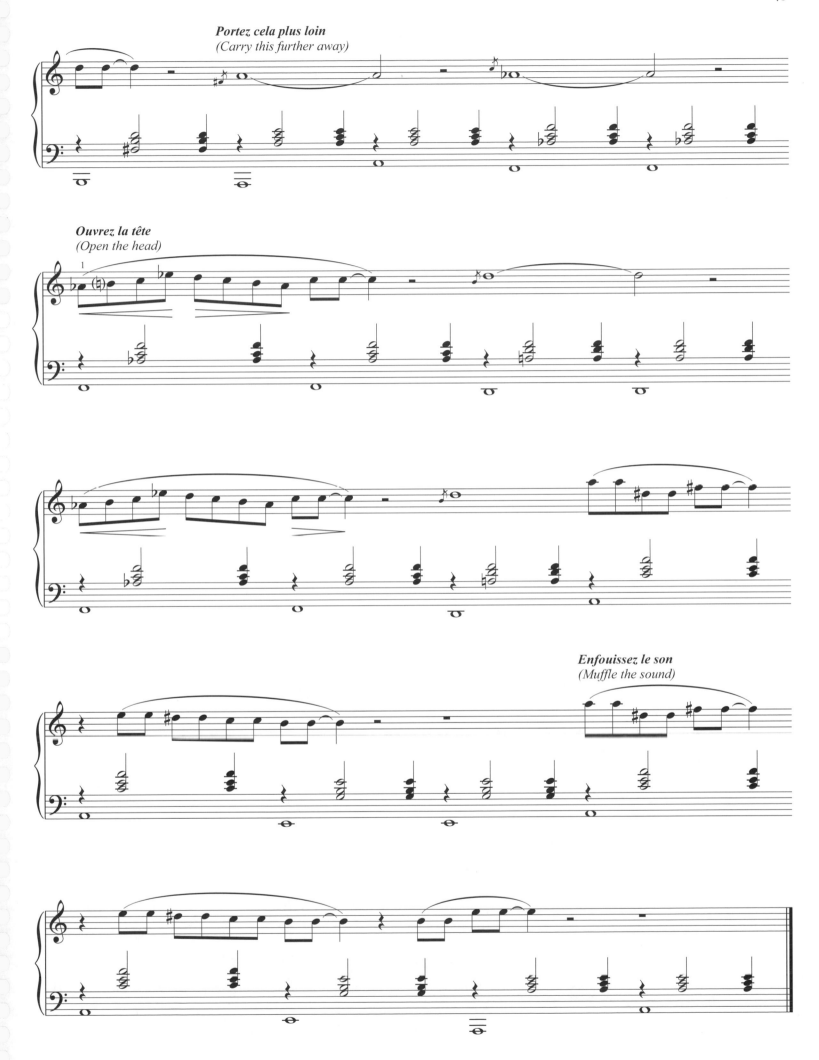

This page has intentionally been left black to facilitate page turns

Gymnopédie No. 1

from *Trois Gymnopédies*

Erik Satie
1866–1925

à Conrad Satie

Gymnopédie No. 2

from *Trois Gymnopédies*

Erik Satie
1866–1925

Lent et triste *(Slowly and sadly)*

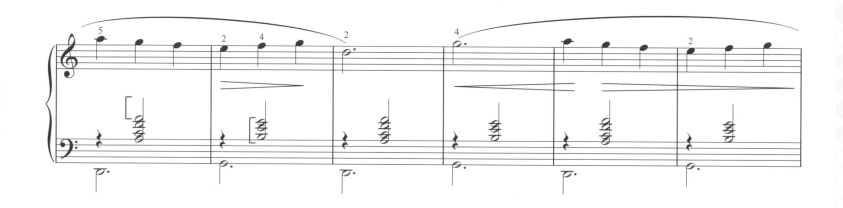

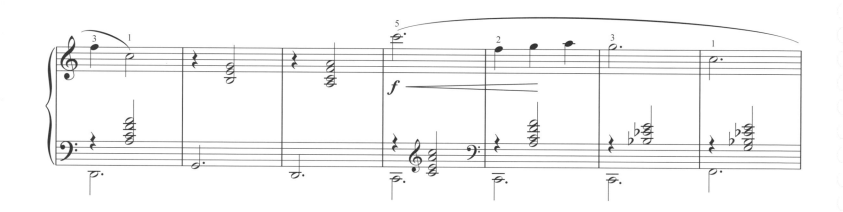

à Charles Levade

Gymnopédie No. 3
from *Trois Gymnopédies*

Erik Satie
1866–1925

Lent et grave *(Slowly and solemnly)*

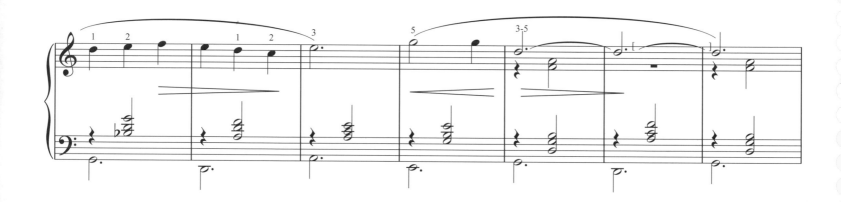